THE WORLD'S
FINAL HOUR

THE WORLD'S FINAL HOUR

formerly published as "Homo Sapiens"

by HAL LINDSEY

A summary of

The Late Great Planet Earth

ZONDERVAN PUBLISHING HOUSE
OF THE ZONDERVAN CORPORATION
GRAND RAPIDS, MICHIGAN 49506

Copyright © 1970, 1971, Christian Information Committee, P. O. Box 4309, Berkeley, California 94704.

Zondervan Books edition 1976
Tenth printing August 1980
ISBN 0-310-27732-9

Published by Zondervan Publishing House,
Grand Rapids, Michigan

Printed in the United States of America

Contents

THE WORLD'S
FINAL HOUR

Homo Sapiens!
Extinction or Evacuation?

We are approaching the most electrifying decade of human history. The 1980s may be the most determinative decade in the history of the human race. The die will be cast as to how history is going to be ended.

We have enough evidence and information available to us today, if we are really honest with what's going on, to show us that man is headed toward some sort of catastrophic climax in his long history. Knowledgeable people are saying that man will probably not survive this century.

Population explosion, pollution, ecological imbalance, nuclear threat — all point to the end.

One scientist recently predicted that by 1980 you will not be able to go on the street without a special breathing apparatus or a gas mask. He stated that air pollution has now reached all parts of the globe — and is increasing at an alarming rate. He said that unless something technologically miraculous happens by 1980, the streets will be largely deserted. Most plant life will be dying, and you will have to have a special air filter to survive in your home. The ecology of the sea is being radically affected and animal life is being radically affected, so that their destruction presents a tremendous threat to our existence.

Population is something else. Scientists say that even if we were to go all out to restrict the population increase, we could only hold the population down to about six billion by the year 2000. Few even try to deal with the problems that would come up in 2015, because, you see, population is increasing on a geometric scale. Every solution I've seen proposed only goes up to the year 2000; no one even wants to think about what's going to happen after that. The reason is that if population takes thirty years to double now, it will take about fifteen years to double again. So man is saying that the most critical crisis the human race has ever faced is the problem of population and the inability to produce food on this planet to feed this vast population.

Dr. W. Stanley Mooneyham in his book, *What Do You Say to a Hungry World?* points out: "But the food crisis does not stand in isolation from the rest of the world's problems. If we were dealing with just an agricultural shortfall, the solution would be relatively simple. But add changing climatic conditions and you complicate the problem. Link it with uncontrolled world population . . . and you further intensify the dilemma.

"Now compound it by introducing ecological factors plus deficiency of medical services, inadequate educational programs, discriminatory distribution systems, global economic inequity and repressive political regimes — add these and you've got an apocalyptic situation."

There is a time limit on the human race from the standpoint of pollution and from the standpoint of population. And there is another great problem we are up against — the nuclear threat. In 1964 Dean Acheson, the former Secretary of State, said, "I know nothing which is classified, but I know enough of what is going on in the world today to assure you that within fifteen years this world will be too dangerous to live in." W. Pickering, former president of the

American Federation of Scientists, said, in 1965, that if we do not find a solution to the nuclear proliferation, there will be a holocaust throughout the world within fifteen years. This continues to be a great threat, and as tension is brought to bear on nations due to overpopulation, due to whole nations stricken with famine, due to air pollution spreading from the more industrially advanced nations to the other nations, the danger of war will increase.

A tremendous increase in population such as we are about to see will simply multiply every existing problem geometrically with it. So crime, lawlessness, and all other social problems will escalate with increase in population. Now it is interesting to note that as you study what scientists and statesmen have said regarding the dangers confronting this generation — they all point to the fact that we may reach a critical point by the 1980s and a catastrophic point by the turn of the century.

All this has caused me to become a "prophecy freak," trying to find out whether the Bible has anything to say about this dilemma. I wanted to know if God has any hope for this generation. I always knew there was a hope for someone, sometime, but I was a little concerned about this generation and not someone way off in the future. Besides, if we are headed toward an obvious climax in history, there must be something in the Bible about it. There are events today which, because they are happening all at once, are different from any other time in history. We are seeing the final fitting together of all the prophetic signs that Jesus said would come.

The First Sign

This one is the most important. If this sign weren't present in the world today, nothing else would be relevant, because every generation has had some of the signs of the return of the Messiah — so that it has always seemed that He might come in that generation. But there never has been a time before this generation when this first sign has appeared. It has to do with God's timepiece, the people of Israel. I am talking about the physical descendants of Abraham, Isaac, and Jacob. About 3500 years ago, Moses made some startling predictions about the future of the Jewish people. These predictions were made at the time when the Jewish people were en route from Egypt to possess Palestine, as God had promised. Moses first predicted that because the people would not believe God and because they would depart from obedience to their God, He was going to scatter them around the world. He said a great nation would come and take them captive, and he said that they would serve this nation and that their own nation would be destroyed.

Now this is the first part of a two-part prophecy regarding their history. Other prophets added details. The dispersion occurred in 600 B.C. when the Babylonians swept in under Nebuchadnezzar and took the Jewish people captive. They annihilated what was left of the nation of Israel, destroyed Jerusalem, wiped out the temple, took the people back to Babylon, and there they stayed — for they were held against their will for exactly seventy years, just as Jeremiah the prophet had predicted (Jer. 25:8-10).

Jeremiah and other prophets predicted that Israel would be allowed to return after that period of seventy years and reestablish their nation. The second part of Moses' prophecy becomes important here. He said first, "You will be taken by a mighty nation," but then he said, "The Lord will scatter you among all people, from one end of the earth to the other. And then you will serve other gods of wood and stone, which neither you nor your fathers have known." As you see, this would be a greater punishment, because he said, "After you return and become a nation, because you will continue to disobey God, you are going to be scattered again; your nation will be destroyed again; only this time you are going to be scattered about the whole world into every nation."

Jesus added details to this prophecy when He was here on earth. As a matter of fact, Jesus told the people, after it was obvious they had rejected Him, "Because you have refused my claims, not one stone is going to be left standing upon another here in the temple." He said that Jerusalem was going to be destroyed and that the people would be scattered throughout every nation. Jesus said this would happen to the generation that rejected Him.

Just as Moses predicted, and as Jesus added in more detail, Titus and the Roman legion swept in upon the Jewish people in A.D. 70 and wiped them out. They destroyed Jerusalem and sold the survivors into slavery; they dispersed them into the world — a dispersion which has lasted up to this present hour.

Moses added more about what would happen after they were scattered. He said, "Among these nations you shall find no ease, and there shall be no rest for the sole of your foot. But the Lord will give you a trembling heart and failing of eye and languishing of soul, and your life shall hang in doubt before you night and day; you shall be in dread and have no reassurance of life. In the morning you shall say 'would it were evening,' and in the evening you shall say 'would it were morning,' because of the dread that your heart shall fear and the sights your eyes shall see." Hasn't that been a history of the Jewish people since A.D. 70? "No rest for the sole of your foot" — that means men without a country, fearing day and night for their lives — oh yes, received for a while with favor, but every nation they have been to has eventually turned against them. And in dread! Moses had predicted this. He said, "This is what's going to happen. Why? Because you're not going to believe your God; you're going to turn your back on God." So he predicted this dispersion.

I want to turn to the essence of this sign. In Ezekiel 36 the prophet predicts that just shortly before the Messiah will return and set up God's kingdom here on earth, destroy evil on earth, and bring about peace and justice, these Jewish people, scattered about the whole world, will be returned and become a nation again. Now remember that as you read Ezekiel 36:16-18, "The word of the Lord came to me: Son of man, when the house of Israel dwelt in their own land, they defiled it by their ways and their doings, their worship being to Me as the uncleanness of a woman in her impurity. So I poured out My fury on them because of the blood which they had shed in the land and for the defilement, which they had brought upon it through their idols" (MLB). (Recall that this is God speaking through the prophet.) God said, "I scattered them among the nations, and they were dispersed over the countries; for according to their ways and their doings, I judged them" (36:19 MLB).

Then in verses 22-24 we have the record that God said after they go through this dispersion, they're going to return. He said, "Therefore say to the house of Israel, Thus says the Lord God: It is not for your sakes, house of Israel, that I am about to act, but for My holy name, which you have profaned among the nations to which you came. I will vindicate My great name, which has been profaned among the nations, and which you have profaned among them; and the nations shall know that I am the Lord, says the Lord God, when, through you, I vindicate My holiness before their eyes. For I will lead you from among the nations, gather you from all countries, and bring you into your land" (MLB).

Jesus the Messiah (before He was taken to be crucified — Matthew 24), as He talked about the things that would be going on shortly before He would come back, told of the return of the Jews to the land of Palestine, as a nation, and He said they would be in possession of old Jerusalem. Now consider that carefully. He also said that the generation who would see the Jews back in their land and in possession of old Jerusalem again would see His return. That is what Ezekiel was predicting 2600 years ago. In the past, many people who studied the Bible would read passages like this which said that God is going to bring the Jew back from his world-wide dispersion and they would say, "This is not literal; this is impossible." Many arguments have been developed on this point which say, "Now it is obvious that the people of Israel could never become a nation again; they have been scattered for two thousand years. So this is a case in point which shows that you can't take prophecy literally."

These things were being said in the 1940s when the indestructible Jews, after being persecuted for nearly two thousand years, suddenly became a nation again in a day, against incredible odds. As you study history, seeing how it happened due to precarious decisions by a few men, Harry S Truman among them, you begin to see that the hand of God was at work behind the scenes. When the Jews became a nation again in 1948, that was the most important sign that any generation could see, because now they had been returned back to their land. It was the first sign.

The Second Sign

The second sign is this: Before the Messiah can come back, the Jew has to possess old Jerusalem because much of the warfare that is to be part of the last war of the world is over the city of Jerusalem. As a matter of fact, Zechariah (in chapters 12-14) writes about the battle of Jerusalem, which is a part of the campaign of the War of Armageddon. And Zechariah 12:2-4 tells us that the last war of the world is going to be triggered over a dispute about who owns Jerusalem. Now mind you, Zechariah was writing 500 years before Jesus was born.

Back in March of 1967 I was invited to speak about Bible prophecy. I said, "If this is the time that I think it is, pretty soon we can expect the Jews to get old Jerusalem." Then came the Six Day War. I believe the whole purpose of the Six Day War was to get old Jerusalem back again. Do you realize that for the first time in 2500 years the Jews have total possession and sovereign control of old Jerusalem? They haven't totally controlled it since they were taken to Babylon by Nebuchadnezzar, and yet they have it now.

That was the second great sign that the world stage was being set for the second coming of Jesus the Messiah. Now, since those two things are true, every other sign I am going to give you has great significance. If those two things were not true, the other signs would not have any more significance than they had in 1940 or any other time before that. But you see, there has never been a time when the Jew has been returned from a world-wide dispersion or been in total possession of old Jerusalem.

The Third Sign

The third sign has not happened yet, but it will soon. The Jew is to rebuild the temple again in old Jerusalem. He has to. In 2 Thessalonians 2 Paul speaks of the great world dictator, the future Fuehrer who is to come. He speaks of his taking his seat in the temple of God and declaring himself to be God. The temple of God can only be the temple in old Jerusalem. Jesus speaks of the environs of the temple in Matthew 24:15-16. He speaks of the "abomination of desolation" which Daniel the prophet predicted. The "abomination of desolation" is a technical

Jewish term. It means the desecration of the holy place in the temple. For the Antichrist to desecrate the temple, there first has to be a temple. I've learned that since 1948 certain Jewish societies have been collecting what they call temple bonds. They already have a tremendous amount of money gathered for the construction of the temple. There were some documents discovered a few years ago, after the repossession of the temple area, which gave the exact methodology of cutting the stone for the temple and so forth. They had been buried for centuries near the Wailing Wall. And now the temple can be prefabricated in about six months — the third sign.

The Fourth Sign

The fourth sign has to do with something that could only happen after the Jews were a nation again in their ancient homeland. In Ezekiel 38, Ezekiel predicts the restoring of the people as a nation. He said that after the Jews are returned from this dispersion, there is going to arise a fantastic power from their uttermost north. This nation would become the arch-enemy of the Jews and this nation would actually be involved in a direct attack upon Israel, triggering the last war of the world. In Ezekiel 38:15-16 we read, "And (you) come from your place out of the far north, you and the many peoples with you, all of them rising on horses, a great host and a mighty army; and you will come up against My people Israel, like a cloud covering the land" (MLB).

We have many clues as to who this power is. They are to the uttermost part of the north from Israel; they will come to power when the people of Israel are returned to their land after they had been scattered throughout the world. So that is the time factor, which is right now. In Ezekiel 38:2,3, this power is addressed prophetically, "Son of man, set your face toward Gog, of the land of Magog, the chief prince of Meshech and Tubal, and prophesy against him. Say, Thus says the Lord God: Look, I am against you, Gog" (MLB).

For centuries, men who have studied this passage have identified who this power is by ethnic background. Meshech, Magog, and Tubal are tribal names in archaeological records that go all the way back to the fifth century B.C. They are tribes descended from Japheth, the son of Noah, and are named in Genesis 10. Herodotus, the fifth century B.C. Greek historian and philosopher, said that Meshech and Tubal were tribes that settled in the northern part of the Caucasus mountains between the Black and Caspian Seas and then fanned out through the northern regions. In the first century A.D., a Jewish historian, Josephus, who was not a Christian, commented on these persons or tribes and said they had scattered out to the northernmost regions above the Caspian mountains and had fanned out to the east to the Siberian plain. He said that the Romans called them Scythians.

I am going to skip over all the documentation I could give and just come down to the first half of the nineteenth century to the writings of William Gesenius, who wrote the greatest dictionary of ancient Hebrew available today. We still base our Hebrew studies on his writings. Gesenius, as he discussed these words in this passage, said, "This is referring to the tribes that now form the Russian people." It is interesting to read commentaries written back in 1711, as for instance that of Bishop Lowth of England, who said this passage refers to Russia and that they would be the great enemies of the Jewish people when God would return them to their homeland. These commentaries tell how they were ridiculed for saying that and how people were saying in that day, "How could those poor peasants over there in Russia ever become the mighty enemy of God that is predicted here?"

But we see in our day these prophecies taking place exactly as they were predicted, because, you see, Russia is the only nation to the uttermost north of Israel. If you take a globe and go directly north, you will end right in the middle of Russia. If you want to read the future of Russia, I can tell you exactly what is going to happen to Russia and its Communist confederacies, because all of its confederates are given here, too. The Arabs are also mentioned.

The Fifth Sign

The fifth sign is that at the same time this northern power will arise, there will come up a confederacy of Arabs who will unite over their common hatred of the nation. Finally, they will actually launch the attack against the nation of Israel, bringing about the last war of the world.

Daniel 11:40-45 gives the battle plan of the first phase of this last war of the world. Starting with verse 36, Daniel leaps to the future; he skips over a big gap of time, and in verse 40 he begins to tell us how the Jewish people will meet their fate in the last days. It says, "At the time of the end." The time of the end is defined for us in Daniel. It is the time when Christ comes back.

The king of the south is also identified for us in this chapter. It is Egypt in league with the Arab nations, and Egypt will be the leader. The king of the south will attack this Jewish false prophet, but the king of the north will rush upon him like a whirlwind, "with chariots, and with horsemen, and with many ships" (this means a great mechanized army with ships), and he will come into the country and will overflow and will pass through. He will come into the "glorious land." The nation of Israel is the "glorious land." Tens of thousands shall fall, but these shall be delivered out of his hand: Edom (that is the modern Jordan) and Moab (that is the southern region to the south of the Dead Sea) and the main part of the Ammonites (that too is part of Jordan). I don't know why they are going to be spared, but they will be.

He (this is still referring to the Russian leader, the king of the north) will stretch out his hands against the countries, and the land of Egypt will not escape. Russia is going to double-cross the Egyptians. He, the king of the north, or Russia, will become ruler of the treasures of gold and silver and all the precious things of Egypt, and the Libyans and the Ethiopians will accompany him — in other words, they will

34

also be captured. But here is something I discovered that was really exciting to me: The words in the Hebrew translated as "Libyan" and "Ethiopian" do not mean what we think of today as the countries of Libya and Ethiopia. These words refer to a whole race of people. The word translated as "Libyan" means the African Arabs — all of them. The word in the Hebrew translated as "Ethiopian" is the word "Cush," which means "black man," and is talking about the Black Africans.

In other words, Russia is going to make a lightninglike thrust, with its confederates, through the Middle East and conquer the whole African continent. (And by the way, this is something that is a part of history. All black men are descendants of Cush, and Cush was one of the first great leaders in all the history of man. So don't think that black men haven't been leaders in the past. The first dictator in the world was Nimrod, who was a black man. He was a strong and intelligent leader. The only trouble was that he was never brought to God.) Then Daniel said, "But (while Russia is doing all of this conquest of the African continent) reports from the East and from the North shall alarm him so that he (the Russian) shall withdraw in great fury to destroy and annihilate many" (MLB). While the Russian army is down in Egypt and Africa, news from the north and from the east will trouble them. If you look to the north of Africa, what do you see? Europe. And as you look to the east, you see Asia.

The Sixth Sign

While all of this is going on, there will be a great confederacy of Asians formed, and they are going to come into this battle once the Arabs and the Russians start a war. Revelation 16:12-14 tells us about their entrance on the scene. The kings of the east will come and position their armies on the banks of the Euphrates River. That river will be miraculously dried up so that this great army can cross and enter into the conflict.

That is the news that will come from the east to trouble the Russians. Revelation 9 tells us in symbolic language that a vast army will come from the Euphrates River. This eastern power will build an army of 200,000,000 soldiers. China, right now, is boasting an army, a militia, of 200,000,000 soldiers. I could never see how China could get an army that size to the subcontinent. Then some years ago I read some news releases and learned that India was taking Pakistan to the UN General Assembly because Pakistan was cooperating with the Red Chinese to build a road over the mountains which separate them, a road connecting the Red Chinese with the subcontinent — a straight shot to the Euphrates River. So this would make it possible to march a vast army from China to the subcontinent through the Euphrates River.

Perhaps the reason Russia could get away with this lightninglike thrust without drawing a counterattack is that the army would have to march a long way. Up to this time, they haven't had the industrial complex to produce a fully mechanized army.

The Seventh Sign

Ezekiel says that news out of the north will bother the Russian leader. That has to do with another facet (a great theme of prophecy). The Bible predicts that ancient Rome will be revived again just shortly before the coming of Christ. Daniel 7:15-25 gives a description of this. In the last days ten nations will rise up out of ruins of the old Roman empire. These ten nations, who will have descendants of the old Roman empire in them, will join together in a confederacy. They will become a vast economic and industrial power. But the real power will come when out of these ten nations, or this Roman culture, will suddenly arise an electrifying leader: I call him the future Fuehrer; some call him the Antichrist. There is a great deal of pertinent information given in the Scriptures about this person, the Antichrist. Scripture says that the ten-nation confederacy, which is basically Western Europe, will come up first; then this dictator will take it over and weld it into a world-conquering power. And for a short while this confederacy will have the whole world under its thumb, until Russia and the Arabs make their attack upon Israel; this starts the disintegration of this world power and causes it to go into the last war.

At the same time that this person rises, there is one who comes up in the Middle East — a great religious leader who is called "the false prophet." He will join forces with this Roman dictator, and he is described in Revelation 13:11-17. These two will work together — one of them is primarily a political leader and the other is primarily a religious leader. I believe we are seeing the stage set for all of this to happen. I believe the European Common Market is the foundation for the revival of Rome and the ten-nation confederacy. Just recently it was announced that soon the Common Market expects to add a tenth nation. I've read many articles on the Common Market which predict that it will become the United States of Europe. A French foreign minister recently said, "The Europe of the future, when it finally unites politically as well as economically, will be the mightiest force on earth."

As soon as these ten nations form the confederacy, the Roman dictator and the false prophet will appear. That means that somewhere in Europe, right now, lives the greatest leader this world will ever know — outside of Jesus the Messiah. Somewhere in Europe there is a man who will make Hitler look like a choir boy. But, this man, according to the profile the Scripture gives him, is going to appear to be the savior of the world. People are going to accept him as a deity and even as a god. He is going to come with an electrifying program; we are even told what the main thrust of his promises will be.

The first promise will be to free the world of war: He will bring universal peace. The second promise has to do with providing an answer to the economic problems plaguing the earth, and that will include the problem of food: He will have genuine answers. But worship of himself will be the price tag. He will force every person in the world to swear allegiance to him as god or they can't receive a number; and if they don't get that number, they can't buy or sell or hold a job.

41

I can see how the stage is being set for that already, because I have read many articles predicting we will have a moneyless and paperless society by the 1980s. I read a report showing how eventually all money and every transaction will be put on computers, and everyone will receive a number. The writers were debating about the best way to keep a person from losing this number, because if anyone found that number, he could wipe you out; he could get everything you had. So they were thinking of tattooing on some prominent place, like the hand or forehead, in ultraviolet letters, a number which would be a lifetime number. Now if that were done, it would fulfill exactly the prophecy about how the Roman dictator will have universal control.

Jeane Dixon has predicted the coming of a great religious leader. She says that this is the strongest vision she has ever had and in her book she talks about the birth of a man who is destined to become a world leader, who will lead the world to peace and bring the world to a one-world religion. Bible prophecy predicts the same thing. The only problem is this: Jeane Dixon says this man will be one of the best men the world has ever known. The Bible says he will be right out of the pit of hell. So this tells me Jeane Dixon's source.

The climax of all I am talking about, when

all of these movements of history will converge, will occur during a seven-year period immediately prior to the return of the Messiah, and Bible students call this period the great tribulation. It will last for seven years. This time is counted off in months and days in Revelation 11.

There is disagreement about just where the Christians will be during those seven years, and my own personal convictions are that if you are a true Christian right now, you will not be here during those seven years, because I believe the greatest and most fantastic event ever to occur on this earth will take place just shortly before the Roman dictator and the false prophet are revealed. In 1 Corinthians 15:51 the apostle Paul said, "Behold, I show you a mystery." (In other words, I am going to show you something never revealed before, something only a Christian can understand.) He said, "We shall not all sleep (sleep is a biblical description for death), but we shall all be changed." The Lord will shout (will give a shout), and we will be caught up in the air and will be changed from mortal to immortal. That means that one second we will be here and the next we will be face to face with the Lord; you will never experience physical death if you are alive at that time. You will be changed from mortal to immortal — never to see death, never to know fear, sorrow, or pain.

You will begin eternity as a king and a priest with Christ forever. And God says He really has an active program for us; heaven is not a place where you sit around in an eternal church service and play a harp. But He says that we are going to be kings, and what do kings do? They rule. We are going to be priests, and what do priests do? They intercede. They are spiritual ministers for some beings to God. So this tells me that maybe God is going to redeem many races or worlds of people on other planets. He says, "He who has been faithful over five things, I will make ruler over five kingdoms. He who has been faithful in ten things, I will make ruler over ten kingdoms." So heaven is not going to be a place where we sit around.

I believe that because of all of these things, we need to take stock of our lives right now. I want to sum up the significance of what's happening today.

Do you realize that Jesus said that the generation that would see all of these things begin to happen would not pass away until all was fulfilled? You are the generation seeing these things; you are the generation which is not going to see physical death. I expect one day in my life to be physically called to see the Lord in the air, without seeing death.

The Bible speaks of the fact that the institutional church will get worse and worse just shortly before Christ takes the real Christians out of the world. All the churches will then be brought into the one-world religion. They are going to be the foundation of a great religion which will be the revival of MYSTERY BABYLON, which was mainly a religion founded on astrology, witchcraft, and, later, drug addiction. In the Book of Revelation we read about a culture of people who are addicted to drugs in a religious sense. This ancient astrological religion will have its world-wide effect, and it is already being set up.

It is very important to note that the Bible says there will be a tremendous number of people who, when they become afraid of all the things they see, are going to respond to the claims of Christ. Just before the taking up of the true Christians, and during the seven-year tribulation, there is going to be perhaps the greatest time of evangelism ever known here on earth.

These new Christians are not going to change the world, because the world is going to hate them and put them to death. We are approaching a time in America when you are going to be killed for being a Christian. It is already happening in much of the world today. Some of you who are Christians may meet the Lord through death, not through translation. The most cowardly Christians will be courageous when the hour of testing comes because the Holy Spirit will not let them deny Christ. We face the hour of the greatest opportunity, because as the world gets darker the light shines brighter.

If you have not yet received Jesus into fellowship with your spirit, you should do so now. In light of the coming events we have outlined, it seems unreasonable to neglect the opportunity God gives you to become a member of His forever family. The invitation is general and the process is simple for those who recognize their need and sincerely want to know Him. John said of Jesus (John 1:12), "all who receive Him, He makes children of God." Those who are His children will one day leave this messed-up world to join Him in looking after the needs of His limitless universe. Why miss it?

This message is explained in much fuller detail and is carefully documented in the book, *The Late Great Planet Earth*, published by the Zondervan Publishing House, Grand Rapids, Michigan.

ORDER
Hal Lindsey
BESTSELLERS

☐	THE LIBERATION OF PLANET EARTH	large paper	$4.95
☐	THE LIBERATION OF PLANET EARTH	pocket book	$2.95
☐	THE WORLD'S FINAL HOUR	pocket book	$ .95
☐	THE GUILT TRIP	pocket book	$ .95
☐	THE LATE GREAT PLANET EARTH	large paper	$3.95
☐	THE LATE GREAT PLANET EARTH	pocket book	$2.50
☐	SATAN IS ALIVE AND WELL ON PLANET EARTH	cloth	$4.95
☐	SATAN IS ALIVE AND WELL ON PLANET EARTH	pocket book	$2.95

Prices subject to change without notice

Buy them at your local bookstore or use this handy coupon for ordering:

Please send me the books I have checked above. I am enclosing $_____
(please add $1.00 to cover postage and handling). Send check or money
order—no cash or C.O.D.'s please.

Mr/Mrs/Miss _____

Address _____

City _____ State/Zip _____

Please allow three weeks for delivery.

Zondervan Retail Marketing Services
1420 Robinson Rd., S.E.   Grand Rapids, MI 49506